How to Work With Your Child's Teachers

DR. CLIFF SCHIMMELS

LIFEJOURNEY
BOOKS

How to
Work With
Your Child's
Teachers

LifeJourney Books is an imprint of David C. Cook
Publishing Co.
David C. Cook Publishing Co., Elgin, Illinois 60120
David C. Cook Publishing Co., Weston, Ontario
Nova Distribution, Ltd., Torquay, England

How to Work With Your Child's Teachers
©1991 by Cliff Schimmels
(This booklet consists of selected portions of *How to Shape
Your Child's Education* ©1989 by Cliff Schimmels)

Edited by Brian Reck
Cover design by Bob Fuller
First printing, 1991
Printed in the United States of America
95 94 93 92 91 5 4 3 2 1

Library of Congress Cataloging in Publication Data
Schimmels, Cliff
How to Work With Your Child's Teachers
Cliff Schimmels
    p. cm. — (Helping Families Grow series)
ISBN: 1-55513-708-3
1. Parent-teacher relationships—United States. 2.
Education—United States—Parent participation.
I. Title.   II. Series:
LC225.3.S343 1991
371.1'03—dc20   91-26536
                                     CIP

Exhibit A. The third-grade students were reading all about planets in their *Weekly Readers*. Since there were various levels of reading competence in the room, the teacher walked quietly about during the silent time. Armed with gentleness and a quick smile, he would stop and help a student through a more difficult passage. Finally, all students had completed the reading and were sitting quietly with their readers folded on their desktops.

The teacher, still mobile and still graciously armed, began to ask questions. At first, only the hands of the brighter, more aggressive students flew to the air of recognition; but soon, the sequence of questions built to a climax as more students began to plead for an opportunity to respond. The teacher went slowly, but with enthusiasm. Each student's answer was rewarded with a comment, a smile, and perhaps an added thought. If a student wanted to add to an answer from one of his colleagues or wanted to ask an additional question, he was given the time and the climate to conclude his investigation. Each child in the room volunteered some kind of oral participation during the lesson.

Time flew quickly. At the conclusion those students could name and spell the planets, place them in their order from the sun, explain their rotation, recite several characteristics about each, and explain the meaning of days and years on earth.

When they were finished, the teacher thanked them for their responses and rewarded each with a Mars bar.

Exhibit B. The algebra class was stumped. The student had just written his problem on the chalkboard. He had shown all the necessary steps toward solution and had circled the number which represented the right answer.

The teacher asked, "Is that the right answer?"

"Yes," the student responded.

The teacher furrowed his brow as if in thought and then asked, "If that is the right answer, what does it mean?"

The student was slightly irritated. "What kind of question is that? I found the right answer; what do you mean, 'What does the right answer mean?' "

The teacher disarmed him with a grin, but continued the questioning. "Students, there are many problems in life which may have a right answer, but just finding it is not good enough. Even though we discover the right answer to the algebra question, we must know why it is the right answer. Now, who can help him out? What does it mean to us that this is the right answer?"

The room was filled with a busy silence. Eyes narrowed as they studied the writing on the board and mouths curled into inquisitiveness. Twenty-nine minds focused on the question, *What is the meaning of the right answer?* The teacher waited patiently for what might have seemed too long for a less-informed educator.

Finally, one student offered a possibility. With gentleness but a commitment to the discovery of meaning, the teacher began the questioning anew. Throughout the rest of the period, the students applied the test of "why" to their right solutions. They confirmed algebraic equations, they pursued mathematical theories, and they pondered the meaning of *meaning*. During that time, there were no discipline problems, no horseplay, no harsh words, and no lack of interest.

Exhibit C. The classroom was in chaos. When the bell rang, the students wandered in, listlessly and casually. Some made it before the tardy bell, but most didn't. The history teacher sat in the front of the room at his desk and called the roll without looking up. After each name was called, a student answered with a perfunctory "here." In a few isolated cases, the "heres" came weakly, after a long silence, accompanied by nervous giggling which certified that it was bogus.

Still sitting, the teacher taught for the day. "Okay. Read the next chapter in your book and answer the questions at the end. We are going to have a test on it Friday."

Someone asked, not completely interested, "Which chapter is it?"

Another student asked, "Do we have to hand in the questions?"

"If you want a grade for them, you do."

Again, a student asked, "Are we going to get back the questions we handed in last week?"

"Yes," the teacher answered.

"When?" It was more of a dare than a question.

"When I get them graded; that's when. What do you people think I am, anyway? I have things to do, too. Now shut up and get to work on the next chapter."

With that, the teacher picked up the sports magazine from his desk and proceeded to flip through it, pausing occasionally to check the progress of the class through the vantage point of his feet resting on the desktop.

A group of boys congregated in one back corner, watching a student carve a dirty word on the desk, talking and laughing coarsely. A small group of girls occupied the other back corner and practiced the art of cosmetics—brushing hair, painting nails, dabbing eye makeup. Two young men sat in the middle of the room and played a computer game. Another student read the newspaper. A few students, scattered throughout the room, silently read the chapter assigned.

TEACHER: THE KEY TO THE SCHOOL EXPERIENCE

Let me assure you that these stories are true. In a one-week period, I observed each one, all in the same district—the latter two in the same building.

What is the point? Simple. Considering the diversity in approaches and in enthusiasm which individual teachers bring to their classrooms, it is rather difficult to make any generalizations about the school system. For the student, the classroom teacher is the school system.

In actual practice, it is a mistake to think of school in terms of a system. I realize the natural tendency to think that way. It is comfortable, particularly if one aspires to be a reformer. It is easy and safe to criticize a system. A system is impersonal. You can blame the system for all your miseries, yet never be faced with the threat of confrontation. No one is the system, so you can even criticize the system to the man in charge without ruffling feelings.

Since the federal constitution is silent about the subject of education, the process becomes, by implication of omission, one of the states' rights under the Tenth Amendment. Thus, there are at least fifty different school systems in the United States. But in each state there are districts—more than 16,000 across the nation—with individual boards, individual needs, individual moods, and individual values; so each district becomes a system. Within each district, each building has a unique personality, a spirit or attitude that makes it a system unto itself. And within each building, each classroom teacher has an individual style, likes and dislikes, specific emphases, a manner of response, a special approach to the art of living.

For your child, the system of education in the United States is defined by what happens in *one classroom*. If that teacher is good, or your child perceives the teacher to be good, then the educational system is good. If that teacher is inadequate and insensitive, then the educational system is bad. It is quite possible for a specific student to go through a school system, from kindergarten to high school graduation, and get an excellent education because he or she, by chance, was always placed in the right classroom. It is also possible that a student could go that same route and never have a really good teacher.

Each year, I ask more than 100 college

seniors why they chose their particular college major (which in many instances is the same as choosing a lifetime profession). More than 90 percent of them give the same answer, "When I was in elementary school [or high school], I had a good teacher in that field." One chance meeting in the schooling process, and an entire life is given direction!

TEACHER: A CONSTANT IN A SEA OF CHANGE

For convenience, educators frequently divide the schooling process into three categorical levels: the principle level, the policy level, and the practice level.

During my twenty years in the educational profession, I have seen changes in the *principles* upon which school officials base decisions. I have seen a greater emphasis on the doctrine of separation of church and state in Supreme Court cases. I have seen restrictions and limitations on school finances. I have seen new attitudes and laws regarding minorities. I have seen changes in course requirements and stiffer teacher-certification standards. For the crusader who carried the cause, each change in principle represented a major achievement, a worthy accomplishment which followed months, perhaps years, of active battle. Yet, in spite of all those efforts, for most children, school is about the same as it was before the battles were won.

During my years in teaching, I have also seen changes in educational *policies*. I have seen the coming and going of dress and hair codes. I have seen the construction and destruction of high school smoking areas. I have seen new emphasis on courses in drugs, economics, values, and driver's education. I have seen an increasing trend to restrict corporal punishment. Yet, school still goes on much as it did 200 years ago.

I have seen changes in educational *practices and programs*. I have seen the modular schedule come and go. I watched the rise and fall of the open classroom. I have heard the proponents and opponents of individual instruction, bicultural education, mainstreaming vocational education, and gifted education. Yet, not all that much has changed.

Despite all the principles, all the policies, and all the programs, the teacher remains the dominant constant in all educational endeavors. Despite all our technology and science, the teaching-learning process is still primarily a human activity. A few highly motivated learners may get some isolated lessons from machines or books, but most of us know most of what we know because someone taught us.

It makes good rhetoric to attack the system, but for the most part the effort is more ambitious than effective. Any real change in the quality of a child's education will begin and be completed not in the United States Congress or in the state capital or in the school board meeting, but in the heart and mind of the *individual teacher*.

THE TEACHER AND THE SYSTEM

Even teachers like to believe in "the system." In most cases, the individual teacher is the key to a successful educational experience and to educational progress. The limits to creativity are in the mind of that teacher in that classroom. Yet, a large percentage will argue vehemently that there is indeed a system and that it prevents them from being as good as they should be. The teachers themselves are the first people who need to understand the guerrilla nature of schools.

Don't get me wrong. I know there are some limitations, restrictions, and rules. I have bumped against a few of these myself from time to time. But there are no rules that demand that any teacher be lazy, rude, unimaginative, or ineffective. These are characteristics of teachers and not characteristics of a system.

When I was a high school principal, we used a standard form for teachers to notify parents if a student was in danger of failing a class. The forms had to go out at least four weeks before the final grading. One day, an algebra teacher came in and asked for sixty forms. Since that represented about seventy-five percent of his student load, I decided to check into the problem.

"Yes," he told me, "they are, in fact, failing algebra."

"But what's the problem? Are they lazy?"

"No," he replied. "They can't do algebra because they can't do simple arithmetic. They can't multiply and divide."

At that particular time in educational history, the report didn't surprise me. Those students had spent their first few years in school during a period of mathematical philosophy which suggested that a child could do calculus before he learned to multiply. Thus, many children didn't learn to multiply.

I thought the solution seemed simple, so I mustered up my best fatherly image, walked around to his side of my desk in an effort to dethrone myself, took a casual pose, and offered some words of great pedagogical wisdom gathered from decades of varied classroom experience. "Why don't you teach them to multiply?"

"But," he answered too quickly, "if I did that, I wouldn't be able to teach algebra."

"Are they learning algebra now?"

"No. Most of them aren't, at least."

"Why not?" This was beginning to sound like a Socratic dialogue.

"Because they can't multiply and divide."

"Well, teach them."

"That takes time."

"Sure it does."

"But then I wouldn't get through the book."

"Who says you've got to get through the book?"

"The principal."

I had him there, I realized—I was the principal. "No. My recommendation is for you to begin where they are, with work they can do, and proceed from there."

"But," he retorted, "if I did that, I

wouldn't be teaching algebra, and that is what I am getting paid to do."

With that, he stormed back to his room and spent the next six months teaching algebra, while I spent those six months trying to explain to parents why their children weren't learning algebra.

That teacher wasn't bitter. He just had a mistaken notion of his task, and he serves as an illustration of the dangers of thinking in terms of a system. In that situation, the system said to teach algebra to freshmen, regardless of individual differences, unique problems, or special needs. The only person who had the power to correct the inaccurate order was the teacher, and he refused to do so. A new policy wouldn't have done much good. A court order wouldn't have changed things that much. Change had to begin in the attitude of that teacher.

I visit scores of different school buildings every year. On those visits I see a variety of funny designs and hear about a catalog of funny rules. But in every building I have ever visited, there are always teachers who are doing a good job of relating to students and are teaching young people the content of effective and efficient living. The individual classroom teacher is still the biggest single issue in determining school excellence in this country.

So we are now back to where we started. If you are interested in rallying around noble causes, getting your name in the paper, and winning battles against an anonymous system, you probably won't find much help in this booklet. But if you are sincerely interested in helping your child survive and perhaps even thrive in this schooling ordeal, and if you are willing to agree that the teacher represents the system to your child, then the following pages may offer help and hope.

EVALUATING, COMMUNICATING, UNDERSTANDING

Like any theory, educational theory isn't much good until it is put into practice. Having a philosophy is important to the teach-er, and eventually to the student, but it doesn't do much good if the teacher doesn't have the enthusiasm, compassion, and intelligence to bring it to life in the class-room.

You need to know how to distinguish between good and bad teaching.

EVALUATING: WHAT MAKES A TEACHER GOOD?

Teaching is a human profession and, as such, it has its flaws and weaknesses. The professional teachers don't endorse these, nor do the administrators; yet they creep in. Sometimes only the students (and their parents, if there are adequate communication channels) are aware of bad classroom procedure. Generally, students are powerless to correct these. If there is to be any improvement, the parents will have to assume responsibility. Christian parents, due to their interest in justice and skill in human relations, are desirable candidates to initiate positive action.

To simplify your task, I submit the following list of characteristics of good teachers. The list certainly reflects my bias, but it is based on years of observation. A teacher's violation of one of these points does not necessarily condemn him or her to the pedagogical junkyard, but these are points to investigate. If too many are absent, you may have a legitimate problem.

1. Good teachers read and hand back homework assignments.
Check your child's homework assignment

each day and ask to look at it when it is returned. If it isn't returned, you probably should start getting concerned.

Some college students who have suspected that their fine writings were going unread have inserted into their papers such sentences as *Underline this sentence if you are still reading at this point.* They then spread the results of the investigation around campus.

I don't recommend deliberate traps, but the point is clear enough. If the work is valuable enough to justify the child's doing it, it is valuable enough to merit the teacher's reading.

2. Good teachers give worthwhile assignments.

A few years ago, I asked an intelligent high school junior to help me one evening. He replied that he couldn't because he had a long English grammar assignment. When I suggested that perhaps I could help, he said no, it was something he had to do himself. I persisted until he showed it to me.

The teacher's objective was to refresh these active, busy, high school juniors on the use of commas. The assignment was for them to copy ninety-six long sentences from a textbook and place commas in the appropriate places. Let me repeat: copy *word for word* ninety-six sentences from a text and insert commas.

I can understand teaching commas. I can even understand asking some students who are having trouble with their writing to copy sentences word for word. But this teacher was dishonest with those students. She should have typed the sentences herself and handed them to the students. This assignment grew out of a teacher's laziness.

Teachers shouldn't waste children's time on busywork. A child's time is precious. There are too many things to learn and too little time to learn them. Look at your child's homework to see whether the lessons to be learned justify the amount of time it takes him to complete the assignment.

3. Good teachers stay in the classroom.

The best way to check this is to listen to your child's stories. If he has too many tales of eraser fights and classroom chaos, the teacher may need to spend more time with the students and less at the coffee machine in the teachers' lounge.

4. Good teachers decorate their rooms.

Most teachers believe that the physical appearance of the classroom is a a part of the instructional process. A room decorated with artwork done by the students themselves can greatly add a to a child's sense of self-esteem.

5. Good teachers are organized.

Good teachers know where they are going. Students in their classes know where they are going. If your child seems to be having difficulty in determining direction or knowing what is expected of him, the teacher may not be preparing sufficiently.

Actually, poor preparation is the cause of many classroom problems. When young teachers come to me and ask for help with classroom discipline, I first ask to see their lesson plans. When a teacher has stayed up late in the night to plan an exciting and valuable lesson, he will probably demand the right to teach that lesson. Your child and every other student will profit.

6. Good teachers communicate with parents.

Teachers complain about not getting parental support, but some teachers forget to ask for it. If you discover that you are not being told about problems or that you are being told too late, you may want to investigate the teacher's energy level.

7. Good teachers don't lose control of themselves.

Interacting with twenty-five defiant youngsters is not a particularly pleasant way to spend an afternoon. Sometimes a teacher reaches his breaking point. I have full sympathy for such a person, and I understand how that can happen. But it can't be tolerated.

Teachers cannot respond to misbehavior with anger, maliciousness, or violence. The teacher must control the situation; but he has no right to ridicule, strike in anger, or abuse a student. There is no room in the profession for teachers who react this way

8. Good teachers don't lose control of the classroom.

For the last ten years the Gallup Poll, as published each fall in the *Phi Delta Kappan* magazine, has indicated that lack of discipline is considered the number one problem in American schools. Lack of discipline is a problem. Rowdiness and destruction are rampant. Schools have initiated a plethora of sociologically and psychologically sound programs in an attempt to restore order. But programs fail when there are no people to carry them out.

There is no single technique or sure-fire method for establishing control, but good teachers will do whatever it takes to remain in charge. Of course, not all silent classes are in control, and not all noisy ones are out of control. A teacher is in control when the students are responding to his direction and objectives for the class.

9. Good teachers give students a sense that the material is important.

If your child rushes home with a burning desire to do homework just as Mrs. Doe suggested, Mrs. Doe is probably a good teacher.

10. Good teachers don't abuse their right to academic freedom.

Each year I go to one of the local high schools and lecture to the seniors. The purpose is purely methodological. The teacher wants to train the students in listening and taking notes, skills which are vital to college success.

Since the objective is method instead of content, I get to pick the topic. I once talked about the history of first-century Rome—a thrilling subject, relevant to dynamic seventeen year olds. I warned them at the beginning that I was going to interject personal opinion and half-truth into the data, and challenged them to sort through this and demand proof.

After talking loud and fast for about forty-five minutes, I gave a short quiz. One of the questions was, "True or False: Rome fell because it did not have a valid program of planned obsolescence."

That question is as loaded as a missile silo. It is a question of economic theory presented as a question of economic fact. No matter how he responds, the student has endorsed an opinion, and his "objective" grade will be based on the opinion he endorses.

This question is illegal. This procedure is illegal. Teachers *cannot* teach this way.

I am a strong supporter of academic freedom, particularly when I can define what it is; but a teacher does not have a right to offend a child. By law, teachers can't teach religion in public schools. By the same law, they can't ridicule it, either. We need to realize that some Supreme Court cases *protect* Christians as well as limit them. Teachers cannot use the classroom for a showcase of personal beliefs, values, or life-styles.

As a member of the human race, a teacher has every right to be what he is. But he cannot use his position of authority to persuade, and he cannot present opinion as fact.

COMMUNICATING: HOW TO GET RESULTS

Just reading the above list isn't going to make you an expert on teacher evaluation. Educational scientists themselves have difficulty agreeing on the difference between good and bad teaching. But you should at least have some idea as to what your child's comments reveal about his teacher. I wouldn't be too alarmed by stories of isolated incidents similar to some in the above list, but if you begin to detect a frequency or a trend, you may need to exercise your right as a taxpayer and concerned parent.

When that time comes, however, it is important for you to do it right. If you make the wrong moves here, not only could you be ineffective, you might be damaging.

So I offer the following list of rules, tempered from a teacher's point of view. I want you to be heard; I want the situation to be corrected; but I think I understand how to speak to teachers in a way that gets the best results.

1. Don't yell "Wolf!"

If you shout too much about every little thing, you will soon develop laryngitis and no one will hear you. Reserve your school visits for significant injustices. If you are fortunate, you may never have to go—at least, not for the purpose of confrontation.

2. Get all the facts.

Sometimes children get so involved in telling a story that they lose sight of the boundary between fact and fiction. And perceptions themselves are distorted in the heat of the moment.

The big boys might not have really set fire to the paper in the bathroom. The teacher may not be as rude as he seems to a fourth grader. These do make interesting stories, and everything your child tells you merits your attention, but just make sure you have both sides of the situation.

3. Try to understand the problem from the teacher's point of view.

A few years ago, I met a teacher who had been highly recommended by both his former and present students. Yet I found him negative, abrupt, and abrasive. I decided the students had overrated him. Later, I learned that his wife had died about a month before our first meeting. The students knew this, and they were willing to allow him time to mourn his loss.

Always remember that there may be extenuating circumstances that must be considered.

4. Go straight to the source.

If the teacher is inadequate, he is the one to whom you need to address the problem. Go to him first. If he doesn't respond, go through the appropriate chain of command. But start with the teacher.

5. Don't put the teacher on the defensive.

Don't go if you are angry. Wait until you cool down and the two of you can discuss the situation calmly.

6. Don't be afraid to compliment a teacher.

You are then in a better position to take issue with him later. A brief note of appreciation for some specific lesson or act can go a long way in making a teacher happier with his salary, and paper isn't all that expensive. Besides, he will get the idea that you have good judgment.

7. Don't make the teacher feel worse than he already does.

If you go visit a teacher for something he has done in a fit of passion, don't be surprised to find him already remorseful. In that case, he needs your friendship, not your sharp tongue. Good teachers sometimes make mistakes, but they are aware of them. They don't need you to point them out.

8. Always approach a teacher with the purpose of correcting the problem.

If the situation gets so bad that you feel you have to make your appearance, don't go with the idea that you are going to get someone fired. Part of the Gospel, the good news of our Savior, is that people can change. As a Christian, your only purpose can be to hope to correct the situation, to make things better for the children in the classroom. And it might not hurt for you to believe in the teacher's ability to improve.

9. Remember individual differences.

The first step in your becoming an educational asset to your child is to become objective about his uniqueness. If you need help understanding this, visit the teacher. He probably has analyzed the situation.

Because of the nature of classrooms, teachers must teach to the norm, the average. If your child doesn't fit into that norm, then that is your problem. He will need your patience and your supplementary help. Don't label a teacher as bad simply because he is not reaching one child.

Don't forget that there are children at both ends of the norm. Your child may need special attention in a specific skill because he has a different learning style. Your child may also need special attention because he learns faster than the normal child. Frequently, the results are similar for both extremes.

Good teachers know these things and see them developing. But unfortunately, when a teacher has thirty unique human creations in a classroom, he simply can't anticipate and correct every tendency.

10. Don't sue.

Look! I'm a taxpayer, too. To sue the public school is to sue yourself. If you have a point to prove, there are cheaper ways to go about it. Check to see how much legal fees have increased in your district's budget during the past five years.

UNDERSTANDING: WHY GOOD TEACHERS WEAR OUT

Every year I teach scores of college seniors who plan to enter the field. Every one of those bright, eager, young people intends to be good. I doubt that there is a weak teacher anywhere who once said during his college days, "I think I'll be a teacher, and I think I will be bad at it."

Sometimes young teachers are not as good as they should be, because they lack experience and adequate preparation. If they survive the first few years without permanently damaging young lives and the American society, they could become good teachers.

On the other hand, teachers frequently start out with a burst of enthusiasm, creativity, and effectiveness, and through the years deteriorate into weak, bland, disinterested teachers. These people don't seem to improve with experience. They just continue to stay in the classroom and dream of retirement in some village which is off limits to anyone below twenty-one.

Those teachers who lose their enthusiasm and effectiveness over a period of years present a major problem to the quality of American education. I don't have some magic solution for reversing the trend, nor do I have much advice for helping renew any specific teacher; but I would like to offer some reasons for this problem occurring. Again, these reasons are from a teacher's point of view, but that view may help you understand some of the pressures which will eventually affect your child's education.

1. Teaching is a continuous-pressure job.

I hear those comments about the long vacations and short days, but teaching is still a pressure activity. A shoe salesman may stay at the store a little longer than a teacher stays at school, but when the salesman goes home at night, he probably realizes he is finished for the day. There is nothing he can do during that time at home to make himself a more effective shoe salesman.

A teacher, on the other hand, especially a good teacher, has very few evenings in his life when he is free from the tyranny of tomorrow's lesson. Regardless of how prepared he may be, he can always prepare some more. There is always another book on the subject which he has never read. There is always a school activity where his students are demonstrating their talents. There are papers to be read, records to keep, plans to be made. For a good teacher the day never ends; he just decides he must quit. In the past twenty years, I have never gone to bed feeling that I have finished for the day.

Some teachers may not always respond to the pressure, but just knowing it is there will eventually make one weary.

2. Good teaching doesn't have many immediate results.

Regardless of what surface reasons teachers use for getting into the profession, most of us had, somewhere in the bottoms of our minds, some idea that we were going to make the world better. And we may be doing that, but it will be at least twenty years before we know. In the meantime, we

busy ourselves with earthshaking issues
such as the difference between a B and a C
grade, gum chewing versus no gum chewing, and the five reasons for the French
Revolution.

While teachers are doing this year after
year, parents watch their children grow
through the impetuousness of childhood,
the awkwardness of early adolescence, the
seriousness of later adolescence, the exper-
imentation of early adulthood, and the
fulfillment of life. If your child makes it
through all these stages and turns out all
right, you are going to rejoice in it—but that
fourth-grade teacher will still be collecting
milk money and settling playground
squabbles.

3. Teachers don't get paid much.

I am not trying to solicit sympathy, but this
is a fact of life. Teachers' salaries are actually relative, according to the local standard
of living. In some places salaries are suf-
ficient to permit the teacher to enjoy a
standard of living equal to most of the
other people in the community. If this is so,
teachers don't really deserve sympathy.

But in many affluent communities,
salaries will not permit teachers the same

standard of living. I don't feel sorry for the teacher; he knew what the salary scale was when he entered the profession. But this lower standard of living also means that the teacher's family must sacrifice because the wage earner chose that profession. At this point in his life, a teacher-parent may get grumpy when he must continuously tell his own children that they can't keep up with the kids down the block.

4. Teaching is an extension of one's personality

I am sure most people have a sense of pride about their work. None of us likes to be told that we are not good at what we do. But because teaching requires so much ego involvement, teachers are very vulnerable to criticism.

I have known some rather competent teachers who have been almost destroyed by critical remarks made by their superiors, their students, or parents of their students. Listening to those kinds of remarks too long will make even the strong become defensive, paranoid, or apathetic.

Teaching is something that involves my personality, my very personhood. If you tell me that I am not a good teacher, you have not merely assessed a skill, you have attacked me as a person.

I have not offered the above list to solicit your sympathy. Nor do I propose that you rush out and start some charitable cause for old, wornout teachers. I simply want to introduce you to the pressures which thoughtful, caring, giving teachers face.

Of course, everyone faces pressures in his work, and there are certainly pressures in being a parent. But if, in your mission to help your child survive and thrive, you ever have to confront bad teaching, you need to have some understanding of those pressures unique to teachers. Without that understanding, there will be no effective communication, and without effective communication there will be no positive change.

I also intend for the above list to lead us to a reassuring conclusion to this sometimes negative booklet. Teachers are human. As such they have weaknesses and they make mistakes. Parents who are interested in their child's education must be alert to the possibility of incompetence and error. But most teachers are actually rather nice people.

Your child's teacher may not be getting the job done. He may be making some noticeable mistakes. But despite all that, he is probably a pretty decent sort. In all my associations with teachers in five states, I have only met a few who were vicious or mean or petty by basic nature, and those people didn't stay in the profession too long.

If you can remember this, you will be more effective as an educational evaluator, you will be more effective as an agent of pedagogical improvement, and you will be more effective as a parent whose primary motivation is to do what is best for your child.

HELPING FAMILIES GROW SERIES

❧ *Communicating Spiritual Values Through Christian Music*

❧ *Equipping Your Child for Spiritual Warfare*

❧ *Family Vacations that Work*

❧ *Helping Your Child Stand Up to Peer Pressure*

❧ *How to Discover Your Child's Unique Gifts*

❧ *How to Work With Your Child's Teachers*

❧ *Helping Your Child Love to Read*

❧ *Improving Your Child's Self-Image*

❧ *Preparing for Your New Baby*

❧ *Should My Child Listen to Rock Music?*

❧ *Spiritual Growth Begins At Home*

❧ *Surviving the Terrible Teenage Years*

ABOUT THE AUTHOR

Dr. Cliff Schimmels knows the school system inside and out. He has been a teacher, coach, principal, pastor, newspaper editor, and is a professor of education at Wheaton College in Wheaton, Illinois. He is currently using his teaching skills on a two-year assignment in the Soviet Union.

Cliff has written an entire series on how you as a parent can help your child get the most out of school. His *School Success Series* includes:
- *It's Time For School*
- *How to Shape Your Child's Education*
- *What Parents Try to Forget About Adolescence*
- *Notes from the World's Oldest Freshman*
- *How to Survive and Thrive in College*